Latimer Briefing 15

How The Anglican Communion Came To Be And Where It Is Going

Michael Nazir-Ali

The Latimer Trust

How The Anglican Communion Came To Be And Where It Is Going©
Michael Nazir-Ali 2013.

ISBN   978-1-906327-18-7

Cover photo: © GAFCON FCA

Published by the Latimer Trust October 2013 with support from the Anglican Association

The Latimer Trust (formerly Latimer House, Oxford) is a conservative Evangelical research organisation within the Church of England, whose main aim is to promote the history and theology of Anglicanism as understood by those in the Reformed tradition. Interested readers are welcome to consult its website for further details of its many activities.

The Latimer Trust
London N14 4PS UK
Registered Charity: 1084337
Company Number: 4104465
Web: www.latimertrust.org
E-mail: administrator@latimertrust.org

Views expressed in works published by The Latimer Trust are those of the authors and do not necessarily represent the official position of The Latimer Trust.

CONTENTS

1. Origins

1.1. Roman and Celtic mission

The origins of the Church in England are lost in the mists of time. The story about the conversion and martyrdom of St Alban, perhaps as early as the third century, gives an indication of the presence of Christianity in the country, albeit in a situation of severe persecution. It seems that the Faith was first brought to Britain by Christians who travelled with the Romans and, it is clear from Bede, that the Britons still retained vestiges of the Faith even after the Anglo-Saxon invasions, although they did not share this with their pagan neighbours.[1]

Such was the situation on the eve of the arrival of Augustine, the reluctant missionary, sent by Gregory the Great and constantly having to be encouraged by him to persist in what he had been sent to do. The English Reformers and monarchs continued to acknowledge this debt to the Church of Rome and to give her all the honour given to her in ancient times, provided she purged herself of the corruption and weakness which had caused the English Church to separate from her. At the same time, however, they pointed out that the Church in Britain preceded the arrival of the Italian mission. Archbishop Matthew Parker is typical in claiming a mythic apostolic pedigree for this Church, but it cannot be doubted that the substance of the claim to antiquity is correct.[2]

The relationship between Roman and Celtic forms of Christianity and between Britain and Ireland is often mentioned and has long been debated. The usual polarisations, however, are not helpful. It should be remembered that Patrick, the founder of Christianity in Ireland, was a British Christian, the son of a deacon and the grandson of a priest. During his exile in Gaul, he became familiar with Roman custom and this seems to have been the form of the Christian faith which he preached. He was, nevertheless, sensitive to Irish spirituality, acknowledging the significance of woods, springs and wells, as well as the importance of dreams and visions. These remain crucial for mission today in many parts of the world.

---

[1] Bede, *The Ecclesiastical History of the English People* (Oxford, OUP, 2008), p 36
[2] See further, Paul Avis, *Anglicanism and the Christian Church* (Edinburgh, T & T Clark, 1989), p 24ff

It is also true, however, that about the same time that Augustine was arriving in the East and the South, Columba, who came from Ireland, not only settled at Iona but also made it a centre for missionary work in the North, evangelising Northumbria, for example, from this vantage point. Monks from Iona, such as Aidan and Chad, continued this mission, renewing the work of Paulinus of York and Rochester which had been interrupted by the defeat of Edwin, King of Northumbria, at the hands of the pagans. Both movements of mission had evangelisation, baptism and Christianisation as their aims but there were significant differences between them as well. While the Roman mission emphasised the organisational aspect of the church in the establishing of sees, the holding of synods and the harmonisation of feasts and fasts, the Celts understood themselves as *peregrini*, pilgrims for Christ. Their primary aim was giving up everything, even their homeland, for the sake of following Christ, but in fact, such pilgrimage was very important for the progress of Christian Mission in early mediaeval Northern Europe. Once again, we find the Irish example was emulated by Anglo-Saxons, such as Boniface, the apostle to Germany.[3]

It should not surprise us, therefore, that there was tension and even conflict between these two forms of mission and of being church. This came to a head at the Synod of Whitby (AD664) and was, according to Bede, largely resolved in favour of Roman customs. In spite of this, we can say that the tension between organisation and movement has recurred throughout the history of the Church: the rise of religious orders, especially the itinerant ones like the Franciscans and the Dominicans, the Missionary Societies and various kinds of para-church bodies all reveal this pilgrim or movement nature of the Church. It may well be that in our own age, which is suspicious of institutionalisation, movements for reform, renewal and community will become increasingly valued.

1.2. Relationship with authorities

While it is true that early mission in England was sometimes supported and even sponsored by rulers, nevertheless, as in the rest of Europe, there was often tension between them and the Church. Although Rome

---

[3] On all of this, see Anton Wessels, *Europe: Was it Ever Really Christian?* (London, SCM, 1994), pp 55ff

prevailed generally in the controversy over the investiture of new bishops by the Crown and although Magna Carta upheld the freedom of *Anglicana Ecclesia* (The Church of or in England), in practice the Crown increasingly restricted the Church's freedom to act, especially, but not only, in the matter of Episcopal appointments.[4] Legislation passed under Henry VIII and Elizabeth I often invoked pre-Reformation provisions like *Praemunire* to prevent interference in the English Church from Rome or elsewhere. Henry certainly acted as 'Supreme Head' of the Church in every way, but his daughter Elizabeth was much more cautious in her claims. Henry's title of 'Supreme Head' was replaced by the more modest 'Supreme Governor' and an Admonition, attached to the Royal Injunctions of 1559, explicitly repudiated any claim by the State to interfere in the ministry of the Church. This is reflected in Article 37 which states that "we give not to our princes the ministering either of God's Word or of the Sacraments ...".[5]

There was a tendency seen in England and elsewhere throughout the mediaeval period, climaxing at the time of the Reformation, of kings seeking to limit the independence of the Church. Whether this leads to a full-blown Erastianism[6] is very much a question worth asking today. The Episcopal theologians Ephraim Radner and Philip Turner have claimed that their church's capitulation to American culture in matters like authority, revelation, the uniqueness of Christ and human sexuality, is an illustration of Anglicanism's 'Achilles' heel', exported to other Anglican provinces by the Church of England. In this context, it is sometimes asked whether the Erastian tendency is not endemic to Anglicanism, found even in its principal expositor, Richard Hooker.[7] This is not to say, as Radner and Turner recognise, that other parts of a broken and divided Church are not also susceptible to an Erastian capitulation.

---

[4]   Colin Padmore, 'The Choosing of Bishops in the Early Church and in the Church of England: an historical survey' in *Working with the Spirit: choosing diocesan bishops* (London, Church House Publishing, 2001), pp 113ff

[5]   Paul Avis, *Anglicanism and the Christian Church*, pp 38f

[6]   Erastianism is the doctrine that the state has full powers over the church in ecclesiastical matters.

[7]   Ephraim Radner and Philip Turner, *The Fate of Communion: The Agony of Anglicanism and the Future of a Global Church* (Grand Rapids, Eerdmans, 2006), pp 2ff and Richard Hooker, *Laws of Ecclesiastical Polity* (ed Arthur Pollard, Manchester, Fyfield, 1990), Bk VIII, pp 191ff.

1.3. Formative influences

The Middle Ages were characterised not only by the struggles between monarchy and papacy and by popular religion but also by movements for reform which sought to return Christians and the Church to a supposed primitive simplicity. The Franciscans are clearly an example of such a movement, encouraging people by their preaching, the practice of evangelical virtues and by their organisation into different forms of common life. Later on, when the old vigour and rigour had been much weakened by worldliness and internecine conflict, these movements themselves became the objects of attacks by newer movements, such as that from John Wycliffe and his followers who, afterwards, came to be known as Lollards. Wycliffe's influence was not limited to England but extended to Middle Europe, through the writings of John Huss. Other movements, like the somewhat mysterious Waldensians, also contributed to the backdrop for the Reformation.[8]

In addition to this, the revival of learning at the Renaissance, encouraged by the development of printing which made possible the wide availability of books, brought into existence a Christian humanism. This varied from place to place but it created a love of knowledge, especially about the Bible and Christian origins, as well as revulsion at superstition and corruption. It is interesting that Erasmus, whose translation of the New Testament triggered so much of the Reformation, was responsible also for a severe critique of popular cults, including that of the Virgin Mary. In his desire to give Mary a truly biblical place in the Church, he was joined by others, such as Sir Thomas More.[9]

1.4. The goals of reform

The early Reformers were quite as exercised as Erasmus and More about the abuses in the Church and it is instructive to compare the language used by More and Erasmus with that of Tyndale. It is a pity that the polemical climate of the time, and perhaps the temperament of the antagonists, did not allow them to see the common ground between

---

[8]   Owen Chadwick, *The Reformation* (London, Penguin, 1990), pp 11ff, *The Little Flowers of St Francis* (London, Kegan Paul, n.d.).

[9]   M. Nazir-Ali and N. Sagovsky, 'The Virgin Mary in the Anglican Tradition of the 16th and 17th Centuries' in A Denaux and N. Sagovsky (eds), *Studying Mary* (London, T & T Clark, 2007), pp 131ff.

them. This is also true of the availability of the Scriptures in the vernacular. Erasmus was an advocate not only of reading the Bible in its original languages but also of making it available to the humblest. Without Erasmus' edition of the Greek New Testament and its Latin translation, Tyndale would have been unable to do his work to make the Scriptures available even to 'a boye that dryveth the plough'. It is to be regretted, though, that Scripture was not generally available in English until the Reformation, in spite of the commitment of Erasmus, More and John Fisher of Rochester that it should be.[10]

The Reformers were, of course, concerned that individuals should come to be right with God but they were also keen that people should lead holy lives and that the Church should be purified. While the radical Reformation may have looked more to a people called out from amongst the nations, the mainstream Reformers were thinking of discipling whole nations by bringing God's Word to them.

1.5. Mission

It has often been said that while the Counter-Reformation featured a great sense of world mission, the Reformation did not. Indeed, it was a common charge against the Reformers that they could make Christians heretics but they could not convert the heathen. Against this, it can be said that the *Padroado* (or *Patronato*), which required Spain or Portugal to carry chaplains with every expedition of exploration or conquest, was inevitably tainted with the cruelty and greed of the *conquistadores*.[11] The religious orders were more independent and while some, certainly, stood up for the indigenous population, others were implicated in their exploitation and subjugation.[12] It can be legitimately said that the renewal of faith, the teaching of the Bible, worship in the vernacular and inculcating a sense of vocation among the laity were the Reformation's focus of mission. It can also be pointed out that, while the sea-routes

---

[10] Brian Moynahan, *William Tyndale: if God spare my Life* (London, Abacus, 2003), David Daniell (ed), *Tyndale, The Obedience of a Christian Man* (London, Penguin, 2000), Eamon Duffy, *The Stripping of the Altars: Traditional Religion in England 1400-1580* (New Haven, Yale U P 1992), pp 53ff and O. Chadwick, *The Reformation*, op. cit., pp 38f.

[11] Michael Nazir-Ali, *From Everywhere to Everywhere: A World View of Christian Mission* (London, Collins, 1990), pp 38ff.

[12] Stephen Neil, *A History of Christian Missions* (London, Penguin, 1990), p 145 and Ondina Gonzalez and Justo Gonzalez, *Christianity in Latin America* (New York, CUP, 2008), pp 73ff.

were controlled by Catholic powers, the Protestant nations could not easily engage in world mission.

Such excuses are not enough, however, for as Warneck, the historian of Mission tells us, no sorrow was expressed in these churches about their inability to engage in mission, and their silence about the missionary task can only be accounted for by the fact that even the *idea* of mission was absent.[13] Bishop Stephen Neill, similarly, tells us that the thrust of Protestant thought was not that missions would come in God's good time but that they were neither obligatory nor desirable. He further identifies this attitude with the Reformation's emphasis on local or national churches. These were not only contained within specific boundaries but were confined to particular ethnicities and to the limited vision of local rulers and populations. In addition, there was a kind of dispensationalism among some which held that the Gospel had already been preached to all nations. There was no need to do so again to those who had refused it before.[14]

There were exceptions, of course, and Neill records some, among them Adrian Saravia, the Dutch Protestant, who became an Anglican and eventually a Canon of Westminster (some say Dean). Saravia believed that the missionary mandate was for every age because it was accompanied by Our Lord's promise to be with his Church to the very end. Such a promise has never been understood to mean he would be with the Apostles only and so the command, to which the promise is attached, could not be limited to the Apostolic Band either. The Apostles, moreover, had chosen fellow-workers and successors to continue their work and, as a matter of fact, the Church's missionary work had continued down the years and more and more people had been challenged by the Gospel, responding to it in different ways. Saravia expressly related his understanding of the continuing missionary mandate of the Church to the doctrine of apostolic succession: bishops were successors of the apostles not only as chief pastors but also as leaders in mission. He was vigorously attacked on the continent both for his teaching on mission and for his view on episcopacy but he remains, for Anglicans, an early champion of mission.[15]

---

[13] G. Warneck, *Outline of a History of Protestant Missions from the Reformation to the Present Time: A Contribution to Modern Church History* (New York, Fleming H. Revell 1901), pp 8ff.
[14] Neill, *A History of Christian Missions*, pp 187f.
[15] Neill, *A History of Christian Missions*, p 189, Nazir-Ali, *From Everywhere to Everywhere*, pp 43ff.

2. Globalisation

In spite of Saravia's courageous upholding of world mission, it has to be admitted that Anglicanism displayed the same lack of interest in world mission as other churches of the Reformation. Even though the 1662 *Book of Common Prayer* provided a rite for the baptism of 'such as are of Riper Years' as useful for the baptising of 'Natives in our Plantations, and others converted to the Faith', Neill can find records for only one Indian being baptised according to Anglican rites in the whole of the 17th century.[16]

So how *did* Anglicanism become global? How is it there is a world-wide Anglican Communion today which is one of the most widely-spread Christian traditions, even if not the most numerous? In fact, there is no single answer to these questions. The Anglican tradition became global in a number of ways. There was, first of all, what we might call the *co-incidental* spread of Anglican churches. Co-incidental in the strict sense of the term, meaning that Anglicanism spread along with the colonisation and settlement by the British of lands in North America, the Caribbean, Africa, Asia, Australasia etc. The colonists, naturally, took their Church with them and, generally, made every effort to see that it resembled the Church at home as much as possible. It is true that already, in this period, the Society for Promoting Christian Knowledge (1698) and the Society for the Propagation of the Gospel (1701) had been founded. Their first aim was to provide for the pastoral care of British people overseas but it was also their desire to bring other peoples, within British dominions, to the Christian Faith. Bishop Stephen Neill records some of the achievements of the German missionaries who worked with these societies of High Church convictions. They ministered according to the Anglican rite and Anglican discipline but never received Anglican orders. SPCK provided the press on which the first Tamil New Testament was printed and it was a SPG-sponsored young man, Philip Quaque, who became, in 1765, the first African to receive Holy Orders according to the Anglican ordinal.[17]

2.1. *The Church Missionary Society and ecclesiology*

The desire for cross-cultural mission, already implicit in the vision of SPCK and SPG, received a huge impetus with the emergence of the

---

[16] Neill, *A History of Christian Missions*, pp 197f.
[17] Neill, *A History of Christian Missions*, pp 197f

Church Missionary Society as a result of the Evangelical revival. The 18th century was a time of great change and even of turmoil in Britain, but it was also an exciting time. The preaching of Whitefield and Wesley had warmed the hearts of many. Bibles were being opened and read with the realisation that God's purposes were universal and that the Gospel had, indeed, to be preached to 'every creature'. Both their Bible reading and their knowledge of Enlightenment thought about the dignity of the person, led many Evangelicals to view the slave trade and the institution of slavery with increasing revulsion. But the Bible also inspired in them a fresh commitment to the world-wide mission of the Church. It is no accident that the Clapham Sect, a group of Anglican Evangelicals, had among their projects not only the abolition of the hated slave trade and slavery itself but also the establishing of a 'model colony' of freed slaves in Sierra Leone. They were also, of course, engaged in improving the condition of the poor in Britain through education, laying the ground work for industrial legislation by their successors, and in what they described as 'the reformation of manners'. The formation of the CMS has to be seen against this background of a Christian mission, influenced by the Enlightenment, but drawing its basic inspiration from the Bible.[18]

From the very beginning the emphasis was on preaching the Gospel, bringing people to personal faith in Jesus Christ and on the emergence of Christian communities that would be self-supporting, self-governing and self-propagating. Where the CMS had to work – by compulsion or by choice – either with the ancient churches, as in India with the Orthodox, or with establishment Anglicanism, it sought the renewal of the Church in worship, theological education and holiness of life. Henry Venn, its Secretary from 1841 to 1872, is usually credited, along with Rufus Anderson, the American mission strategist of the same period, and then later Roland Allen, from a more High Church background, with the formulation and development of the 'three-self' principle. As Peter Williams has shown, however, they were not unique in such thinking since other Anglicans, Protestants and Roman Catholics also thought in similar ways.[19]

---

[18] As the background to all of this, see David Bebbington, *Evangelicalism in Modern Britain* (London, Unwin Hyman, 1989), Kevin Ward and Brian Stanley (eds) *The Church Mission Society and World Christianity 1799-1999* (Grand Rapids, Eerdmans, 2000) and Jocelyn Murray, *Proclaim the Good News: A Short History of the Church Missionary Society* (London, Hodder & Stoughton, 1985).

[19] Peter Williams, *The Ideal of the Self Governing Church: A study in Victorian Missionary Strategy* (Leiden, E.J. Brill, 1990), pp 1ff.

In the Anglican context, however, CMS did insist on the priority of a Christian community over the need for bishops. In a characteristic dispute with the Tractarians,[20] it rejected the need for 'missionary bishops' who would then establish a church with clergy, appropriate church government, discipline and so on. As Williams has shown, this ideal was compromised from time to time but it remained a basic ecclesiological difference between CMS and the more High Church societies, such as SPG and the Universities Mission to Central Africa (UMCA), as well as with colonial bishops like Bishop G S Selwyn of New Zealand and then of Lichfield. It cannot be claimed that CMS's motives in promoting such an ecclesiology were entirely disinterested. It feared the appointment of High Church bishops and the possible curtailment of its own rôle as a voluntary mission organisation. How ironic, therefore, that the first appointment of missionary bishops in our own times should take place in Nigeria, one of the first areas of operation for the CMS.[21]

Venn and therefore CMS were firm advocates of the emergence of independent national churches which were to enjoy the closest spiritual relationship with the Church of England but would otherwise be responsible for their own worship, discipline and order.[22] In this sense, they have also sown the idea of 'autonomy' which both characterises contemporary Anglicanism and has become its leading problem.

2.2. *Fundamental principles: the Word of God*

Almost from the beginning, the Evangelical Movement had a vigorous debate about the nature of the Bible. All agreed that the Bible was, indeed, the inspired Word of God but differed in their understanding of such inspiration and its extent. Thus some could, and did, refer to it as 'the infallible Word of God'. Then there were those, like Philip Doddridge, who distinguished between different degrees of inspiration

---

[20] See further pg 12 below.
'The ideas of the Oxford movement were published in 90 Tracts for the Times (1833–41), 24 of which were written by Newman, who edited the entire series. Those who supported the Tracts were known as Tractarians who asserted the doctrinal authority of the catholic church to be absolute, and by "catholic" they understood that which was faithful to the teaching of the early and undivided church. They believed the Church of England to be such a catholic church.' (*Enclyclopaedia Britannica*)

[21] Williams, *Ideal of the Self Governing Church*, pp 11ff

[22] Williams, '"Not Transplanting": Henry Venn's Strategic Vision in Ward and Stanley', *Ideal of the Self Governing Church*, pp 147ff

since, for him, some parts afforded a greater insight into the divine mind than others. And, yet again, there were those, such as Henry Martyn, the well-known missionary and translator, who explained to a Muslim interlocutor that, in contrast to what Muslims believed about the Qur'an, he believed that, for the Bible, the 'sense was from God but the expression from the different writers of it'. The fault lines were thus laid for the bitter controversy which was to break out from time to time.[23]

There were several periods and aspects to this controversy but, for our purposes, it was the division within CMS (sometimes called 'the barometer of Anglican Evangelicalism') which is relevant. There was, first of all, the direct issue of the historical trustworthiness of the Scriptures. A significant number of the CMS membership felt that missionary candidates should be made to subscribe to some formula which expressed this clearly. Others, including CMS staff, held that candidates should not be asked to believe in anything beyond the formularies of the Church of England. Behind this lay the ubiquitous issue of 'Anglican comprehensiveness'. Should CMS strive to be as comprehensive as the Anglican Church and, if not, what were the limits?

In the end, a formula could not be found to keep both sides together and this led to the formation of the Bible Churchmen's Missionary Society consisting of those who wished to uphold the trustworthiness of Scripture in every respect and not just in matters of faith. This division in Evangelical missionary ranks was a heavy blow at the time, but, in due course, the formulation of the BCMS provided another opening for those wanting to engage in world mission. BCMS set out to be a pioneer in a number of areas and eventually some of its work became complementary to CMS. Much of the bitterness was forgotten but the question about the nature and extent of biblical authority still lurks in the background.[24]

2.3. The impact of volunteers

An important aspect of mission and the Evangelical revival is its voluntary aspect. The labours of the Clapham Sect, the rise of CMS and other features of the revival can perhaps best be described as

---

[23] Bebbington, *Evangelicalism in Modern Britain*, pp 12f, 86f
[24] Bebbington, *Evangelicalism in Modern Britain*, pp 217f, Murray, *Proclaim the Good News*, pp 177ff

expressions of a voluntary movement of Christians concerned for justice and freedom, for instance with regard to slavery and the working conditions of men, women and children, but also concerned to bring the Gospel to people both at home and abroad. The CMS was always keen to emphasise the 'Church' aspect of its identity and that this was approved by the wider Church is shown by the fact that, throughout the 19th century, more and more bishops agreed to become Vice-Presidents of the Society.[25] At the same time, it and other organisations also wished to affirm the voluntary nature of their calling which distinguished them from, for example, the High Church SPG which had been established by Convocation and by Royal Charter. At a time when institutional provision seems to be failing the Church, the idea of men and women being called by God for mission and ministry is becoming attractive once again. It is very instructive, in this context, to consider the history of voluntary movements in the Anglican Communion and the wider Church.

2.4. The Society for the Propagation of the Gospel

The older missionary societies, SPCK and SPG, were founded on High Church (rather than CMS's 'Church') principles but, as Bishop Stephen Neill points out, until 1861, they had no scruples over employing non-episcopally ordained German Lutherans to minister according to the Anglican rite in the areas of their mission activity.[26] This would not be possible after the Tractarian movement had begun in the Church of England.

One of its more recent historians, Bishop John Davies, comments that Mission was not, at first, a priority for the leaders and thinkers of the Oxford Movement. They were more concerned with questions about the nature of the Church and its relations with the State, with the Sacraments and the ministry which made them possible. Already, in the early period, however, leaders like Hurrell Froude and John Henry Newman were becoming attracted to the idea of being missionary bishops abroad where they could develop their ideas about

---

[25]   Williams, *Ideal of the Self Governing Church*, p14 footnote 118
[26]   Neill, *A History of Christian Missions*, pp 198f

the Church and its oversight free of what they regarded as the 'Erastian' constraints of England.[27]

The real catalyst was David Livingstone's speech at the Senate House in Cambridge in 1857. Among other things, it led to the formation of the Universities Mission to Central Africa. It is, indeed, remarkable that such an Anglo-Catholic mission should have begun under the inspiration of, and with the actual assistance of, a Scottish Congregationalist. The Mission was, from the beginning, characterised by an emphasis on missionary bishops and on seeing the Church as first and foremost a spiritual society. It was active against slavery and, as Neill points out in his book on Anglicanism, no-one can fail to be moved when they see the cathedral in Zanzibar built on the very site of the old slave market and with its sanctuary where the whipping post had been. It is interesting to note, in this context, that the first African to be ordained, as a result of the Mission's work, was a former slave of the Sultan of Zanzibar.[28]

The SPG was also gradually 'catholicized' and became, in many ways, characteristic of Catholic Anglican mission values. The merger of the two societies in 1965 to form the United Society for the Propagation of the Gospel can be seen as a kind of watershed in the story of Anglican Catholic Mission.

2.5. A World-wide Anglican communion

Anglicanism then became a world-wide communion in at least three quite distinct ways.

That is to say, it spread *co-incidentally* (in the strict sense of that term) alongside the movements of English-speaking peoples across the world; into the Americas, the Caribbean, Africa, Asia and the Pacific. As these people went to new lands, they took their church with them. Not only were buildings and architecture transplanted, but also ways of worship, styles of church government, the temper of pastoral care and so on. In some parts of the world, the tendency to replicate what was at 'home' was more pronounced than in others but, on the whole, this

---

[27] Williams, *Ideal of the Self Governing Church*, pp 13f, John D. Davies, *The Faith Abroad* (Oxford, Blackwells, 1983), pp 1ff.

[28] Neill, *Anglicanism* (Harmondsworth, Middx, Penguin, 1958), pp 342f and *A History of Christian Missions* pp 265ff, 323ff.

kind of Anglicanism looked much like its mother, the Church of England, even when events, like the American Revolution, modified some of its features.

The other great force was the *Evangelical* revival and the birth of societies like the CMS, the Church's Ministry amongst the Jewish people and the participation of Anglicans in inter-denominational ventures, such as the Bible Society. The emphasis here was on personal conversion, the planting of Christian communities and the centrality of the Word of God. Church order was deemed secondary and was to follow the establishing of churches. The aim was that these should be self-supporting, self-governing and self-propagating.[29] Evangelical Anglicans were willing to enter into 'comity' arrangements (demarcating areas of mission work) with non-episcopal churches and these arrangements still determine the ecclesiastical map of many countries in Africa and elsewhere.[30] They also became the occasion for discussions about greater Christian unity and led, in some places, to schemes for united churches.

By contrast, the Anglican *Catholic* missions were concerned to uphold the distinctiveness of Anglican Church order and tended to see world mission as a way of establishing authentic 'catholic' order in the unambiguous way that was not possible in the Established Church. Their concern for the Church's freedom and their belief that it was primarily a spiritual society had led Anglo-Catholics from the very beginning to be suspicious of, even hostile to, the Establishment.[31]

2.6. Church-State relations

It is claimed sometimes that there is an inherent tendency to Erastianism amongst Anglicans, and that the tendency to compromise with or capitulate to culture is Anglicanism's Achilles heel.[32] It cannot be denied that the Church of England's relations with the State have

---

[29]   See further Bebbington, *Evangelicalism in Modern Britain*, pp 2ff and Williams, *Ideal of the Self Governing Church*, pp 2ff and *passim*.

[30]   Neill, *A History of Christian Missions*, p 401, Murray, *Proclaim the Good News*, pp 170f

[31]   Davies, *The Faith Abroad*, pp 42ff.

[32]   For a critique of the Erastian tendency, see David Nicholls and Rowan Williams, *Politics and Theological Identity* (London, Jubilee Group, 1984) and on compromise with culture see Ephraim Radner and Philip Turner, *The Fate of Communion: The Agony of Anglicanism and the future of a Global Church* (Grand Rapids, Eerdmans, 2006), pp 2f.

often encouraged a theology and praxis which legitimises the *status quo*. There are, undoubtedly, those, in both Church and State, who regard Establishment as a licence by the State for the Church to exist and to enjoy certain privileges. Nicholls and Williams (see footnote 32) point out that this was certainly not the original meaning of being established by law, however it may have come to be understood down the centuries.

It is then something of a surprise to many when they learn that in fact there are well-established traditions of being prophetic and even of dissent within Anglicanism. We see this in St Anselm's insistence that Henry I should take an oath to maintain the liberties of his subjects before he could be crowned, St Thomas Becket's sacrificial championing of the Church's freedoms or Stephen Langton's leadership against King John in upholding Magna Carta. This shows us how principled resistance could take place in the Pre-Reformation *Ecclesia Anglicana*. At the time of Henry VIII's claim to Royal Supremacy over the Church, the not-wholly courageous Convocations accepted Henry's claims only 'insofar as the law of Christ allows'. The martyrdoms, on both sides of the Reformation divide, showed how people of every rank were prepared to suffer and even to die for their convictions.[33]

The Puritans did not believe that either Edward VI or Elizabeth had completed the task of the Reformation. In this sense, they wanted the Reformation to continue until the Church had been purged of all corruption, error and idolatry. Nothing should be done which was not explicitly laid down in the Bible and they wished such high-mindedness not only for the Church but, by force of law, for society at large. Their austere view of the Christian life was resented by many which, no doubt, accounts for the pejorative way in which the term is understood today. This is not the place to discuss the merits or otherwise of their agenda, save to say that it inevitably involved them in resisting and opposing authority.[34]

In many ways, the Non-Jurors were the exact opposite to the Puritans. They were High Churchmen who also believed in the Divine Right of Kings. Paradoxically, it was this very doctrine which brought

---

[33] On all of this, see further Catherine Glass and David Abbott, *Share the Inheritance* (Shawford, Hants, The Inheritance Press, 2010), pp 33ff and Owen Chadwick, *The Reformation* (London, Penguin, 1990), pp 99f, 125ff.

[34] Chadwick, *The Reformation*, pp 175ff and A.M. Renwick and A.M. Harman, *The Story of the Church* (Nottingham, IVP, 2009), pp 130ff.

them into conflict with the State and the monarch. Having taken oaths of allegiance to the exiled James II and his successors, they were unable to take even modified oaths to the newly arrived William and Mary. Because of this, the bishops (including the Archbishop of Canterbury) and the clergy among them were deprived of their sees or their livings by Parliament without there ever having been canonical proceedings against them. Some formed communities of their own, while others continued to worship in their parish, even if they were unable to hold any office in the official Church of England. Some of the bishops wished to ensure ministerial succession since they increasingly saw the official Church as hopelessly compromised. They also desired to worship in the way they imagined the 'primitive' Christian communities to have done. Eventually, they produced a Eucharistic rite, which showed signs of Eastern influence (as they were also engaged in negotiations for union with the Eastern Churches). This rite influenced the liturgical tradition of the Scottish Episcopal Church and, through it, has been significantly influential in other parts of the Anglican Communion, thus providing an alternative liturgical tradition to the English *Book of Common Prayer*.

The Non-Jurors were not just scrupulous about their oaths. Their negotiations with the Orthodox reveal their sense that they belonged to a world-wide Church and that this somehow had to be visible. They believed the Church to be a distinct spiritual society which, while owing obedience to the State, could not obey if the State demanded something that was contrary to God's Law and its own integrity.[35]

As we have seen, the Tractarian movement also arose because of unease with the State's intervention in the affairs of the Church. Its prophetic stance, however, went beyond the assertion of the Church's independence *vis-à-vis* the State. It extended to crossing social and cultural boundaries, especially to working amongst the poor. The work of priests, like Fr. Charles Lowder in the East End of London, is well-known. Alongside them were orders of nuns like the All Saints' Sisters of the Poor and the Sisters of St John the Divine, now made famous by the BBC's series *Call the Midwife*. Although such work could simply be ameliorating the lot of the poor and at times could be naïve and patronising, there was no doubt about their commitment to live among the poor and to bring their plight to the attention of those who had the

---

[35] Michael Nazir-Ali, *From Everywhere to Everywhere*, pp 51f

power to change it for the better. It is also undoubtedly the case that some struggled for justice for the poor and suffered for it.[36]

Although the prophetic aspect of Catholic Anglicanism has receded somewhat in the United Kingdom in recent years, it has been to the fore elsewhere. For example, at least part of the cause of the Church of the Province of Southern Africa's stand against colonialism, Civil War and, in particular, the abhorrent doctrine of apartheid was the Catholic background and formation of that Church.

We can see then that although there *are* elements in Anglicanism which can lead to compromise with and capitulation to culture and to the demands of the State, there are other forces which can provide the wherewithal for resistance and a counter-cultural stance, if that becomes necessary.

2.7. Differing emphases of a broad church

The different strands of Anglicanism were to be found side by side in some parts of the world. In India, for example, there was, first of all, the Ecclesiastical Department of the Government of India. The bishops were 'Crown' bishops and their task, with their clergy, was to look after the British in India: civil servants, soldiers, traders and so on, as well as a growing Anglo-Indian population. Large churches, in Gothic or Anglo-Moorish style, were built in the European areas of towns and cities, particularly the cantonments. The churches reflected the might and the wealth of the Raj but have now to be maintained by denominations and congregations that are much poorer. Some of the chaplains did have a burden for reaching out to Indians but that was not their primary responsibility. There was then the 'Evangelical' wing of Anglicanism, with churches and institutions emphasising not only the necessity of personal conversion but also the centrality of the congregation in the life and mission of the Church. This was accompanied by the more 'Catholic' presence of the SPG, with an emphasis on an Apostolic ministry, the contextualisation of liturgy and the centrality of the bishop in the Church's work. Bishop Stephen Neill

---

[36] R. Williams, *Politics and Theological Identity* pp 19f, Lawrence Osborn, 'Care and Change in our Society' in Ian Bunting (ed), *Celebrating the Anglican Way* (London, Hodder, 1996), p. 174, Peter Mayhew, *All Saints: Birth and Growth of a community* (Oxford, All Saints, 1987), and Jennifer Worth, *In the Midst of Life* (London, Phoenix, 2010).

has noted how the two societies worked side by side, with tensions and rivalries but also with a spirit of cooperation and partnership.[37]

India was not alone in having these different expressions of Anglicanism present at the same time and, sometimes, in the same place. In some cases the situation was even more polarised. In what is now Tanzania, for instance, part of the area was evangelised by the Anglo-Catholic UMCA and part by the avowedly Evangelical BCMS.

2.8. The basic unit of the church

When it came to 'diocesanisation' and later 'provincialisation', these different expressions had to be brought together into a coherent whole. Constitutions had to be agreed, canons promulged and liturgies produced which would reflect each of the traditions but would also be rooted in history and, most importantly, in the culture of the peoples to whom the Church ministered. In different parts of the world, these processes were not without pain but, in the end, they provide a recognisable Anglicanism which was yet aware of its diverse cultural settings.[38]

There continues to be vigorous debate about the basic unit of the Church. Is it the congregation, the bishop with clergy and people (the diocese) or is it a Province (like the Church of England, Nigeria, etc)? In the Church of England, the size and the bureaucratic nature of the diocese works against it being seen as an effective ecclesiastical expression. Congregations, especially large Evangelical ones, are pressing their claims, more and more, to being regarded as the basic unit of the Church. They claim they have all the necessary elements to be regarded as such: preaching the pure Word of God, the administration of the Sacraments and ministries of oversight.

In the New Testament, the Church of God in Corinth, Ephesus or Rome certainly appears to be a basic way of referring to the Church: all of God's people gathered together in a particular locality (while at the same time, recognising groups of Christians affiliated to particular households. Thus in the Letters to the Romans and the Colossians, St Paul can ask the wider Church to greet the Church in the house of Prisca and Aquila or in that of Nympha). The letters of Ignatius show that early in the 2nd century in, at least, some parts, bishops gathered

---

[37] Neill, *A History of Christian Missions*, p 232
[38] See Michael Nazir-Ali 'The Vocation of Anglicanism', in *Anvil* Vol 6, No 2, 1989 pp 115f

with clergy and people had become a basic way of understanding the Church (though we must remember that we are still speaking of a single town-wide congregation).

The New Testament also recognises the affinity which churches in a region may have for one another (2 Corinthians 8, Colossians 4:16, I Peter 1:1, Revelation 1:4 etc). This, in fact, may be the germ of the provincial idea which is then developed in the East in the sense of bishops grouped around a Metropolitan and in the West in the form, for instance, of the North African Church. The former development is attested to in the Canons of the Council of Nicaea and the latter in the letters of Cyprian, especially to successive bishops of Rome.[39]

I have often had cause to remark how Anglicanism at its best, whether deliberately or accidentally, can display a 'Cyprianic' ecclesiology which emphasises not only the unity and equality of the bishops but also the proper autonomy of provinces – without, however, jeopardising the communion that local churches need to have, if they are authentically to be 'church' with churches throughout the world.

3. A united Communion

The Reformation in England had rejected Cyprian's view that the See of Rome was, at least, the means of establishing communion among the churches and had firmly established the principle of provincial autonomy. As the Anglican Communion emerged, however, questions arose as to how it was to be held together. The development of the so-called 'Instruments of Communion' came about as an answer to this question.

3.1. Lambeth

The Archbishop of Canterbury has always been seen as *primus inter pares* in the world-wide college of bishops and as able to gather together the bishops of the Communion. When bishops in Canada, the USA, the Caribbean and South Africa petitioned for a synodal gathering, the Archbishop of Canterbury responded by summoning the Lambeth

---

[39] W.H.C. Frend, *The Early Church* (London, Hodder, 1965), pp 154f and Robert B. Eno, *Teaching Authority in the Early Church* (Wilmington, Delaware, Michael Glazier, 1984), pp 84f.

Conference. For reasons largely to do with the Establishment of the English Church, he could not summon a proper synod but rather a somewhat attenuated meeting for 'brotherly counsel and encouragement'.[40] Since then, the Conferences have had, nevertheless, a significant influence within the Communion and beyond. Thus the 1888 Conference formulated the definitive version of the Chicago-Lambeth Quadrilateral which set out the basis for Christian unity as being the final authority of the Bible, the Catholic Creeds, the dominical sacraments of Baptism and the Supper of the Lord and the Apostolic Ministry.[41] It is impossible to overstate the importance of the Quadrilateral, not only in Anglican negotiations with other churches, especially after Lambeth 1920's *Appeal to all Christian People*, but also in the wider Christian body generally. It cannot be imagined that the schemes for organic unity, such as that in South Asia, West and East Africa, England and Wales could even have been drawn up, let alone come to fruition as they did in South Asia, without this short but definite formula. Its influence is not, however, limited to such schemes but extends to the Faith and Order Movement more generally and, in particular, to documents such as the Lima Text, *Baptism, Eucharist and Ministry*, of the World Council of Churches' Faith and Order Commission.[42] More latterly, as Bishop Arthur Vogel has pointed out, the Quadrilateral has increasingly been seen not just as a 'yardstick' which Anglicans apply to ecumenical discussions but as a 'mirror' which shows up our own short-comings and what we are called to be as a Communion of churches.[43]

As we have seen, Lambeth Conferences have provided ecumenical guidance about schemes for unity with other Christian traditions but they have also become important for evaluating bilateral

---

[40] Neill, *Anglicanism*, pp 358ff and Alan Stephenson, *Anglicanism and the Lambeth Conferences* (London, SPCK, 1978), pp 30ff.

[41] See G.R. Evans and J Robert Wright, *The Anglican Tradition: A Handbook of Sources*, (London, SPCK, 1991), pp 354f.

[42] On Church Union see Evans & Wright, *The Anglican Tradition*, pp 412f, W.J. Marshall, *Faith and Order in the North India/Pakistan Unity Plan* (London, Friends of the CNI, 1978) and *Ministry in a Uniting Church* (Swansea, Commission of the Covenanted Churches in Wales, 1986). On the wider influence see Günter Gassmann, 'Quadrilateral, Organic Unity and the WCC Faith and Order Movement' in J Robert Wright (ed) *Quadrilateral at One Hundred*, (Cincinnati, Ohio, 1988). For the Lima Text, 'Baptism, Eucharist and Ministry', *Faith and Order* Paper No 111 (Geneva, WCC, 1982).

[43] In Wright, *Quadrilateral at One Hundred*, pp 126ff.

ecumenical agreements such as the ARCIC Final Report.[44] Nearly every Conference until 2008 also provided some spiritual and moral guidance on crucial issues of Christian living, whether it was contraception (1930), racial discrimination (1948) or The Family (1958) right up to 1998 on Human Sexuality. It is sad to record that the 2008 Conference was not allowed to offer any guidance or to make any decisions, thus interrupting the flow of doctrinal, personal and social teaching.[45]

3.2. Fragmenting meetings of bishops

The Lambeth Consultative Body was a meeting of bishops representing their respective provinces and churches which went back to the Lambeth Conference of 1897. It was to meet yearly and would provide for continuity between Lambeth Conferences. In addition, the 1948 Conference recommended the setting up of an Advisory Council on Missionary Strategy. Both the Primates' Meeting, as one of the Instruments of Communion, and the Anglican Consultative Council have emerged as a result of these bodies.[46]

The Anglican Consultative Council is a somewhat strange animal. Its membership consists of bishops, clergy and lay people, nominated by each province, in proportion to its size but it is not itself synodically constituted. That is, it does not have 'houses' for bishops, clergy and laity which could exercise a rôle proper to them in making decisions, particularly about the doctrine, worship, order and moral teaching of the Church.[47]

At the same time, we need to note that both the 1988 and the 1998 Conferences, sensing the need for greater spiritual and moral guidance for the Communion, had asked for an enhanced rôle for the Primates' Meeting.[48] The Windsor Report recognised this special rôle for the Primates, as did the earlier drafts of the ill-fated Anglican Covenant. Under pressure, however, from the very provinces which had

---

[44] See, for instance, *The Truth Shall Make You Free, Report of the Lambeth Conference 1988*, (London, ACC, 1988), Res 8, pp 210f.

[45] Roger Coleman (ed), *Resolutions of the Twelve Lambeth Conferences: 1867-1988* (Toronto, Anglican Book Centre, 1992).

[46] Stephenson, *Anglicanism and the Lambeth Conferences*, pp 122f, 252f.

[47] Coleman, *Resolutions of the Twelve Lambeth Conferences*, pp 171f.

[48] *The Truth Shall Make You Free*, Res 18, p 216 and *The Official Report of the Lambeth Conference 1998* (Harrisburg, Penn, Morehouse, 1999), Res III.6, pp 396f.

made the drafting of a covenant necessary, this was abandoned and replaced by a process which would, once again, make effective discipline virtually impossible.[49]

For the 2008 Lambeth Conference, the Archbishop of Canterbury was unable to gather all the bishops since more than a third refused to come. This was because those bishops who had laid hands on a person in a same-sex partnership to make him a bishop, had also been invited without being required to express regret or repentance for their actions. A significant number of Primates now refuse to attend Primates' Meetings for similar reasons, thus making it impossible for such meetings to be held. Again, for principled reasons, a number of Primates, bishops and lay people have resigned from the Anglican Consultative Council and the Joint Standing Committee of the ACC and the Primates' Meeting.

3.3. The emergence of unifying movements

The result of all of this has been that none of the 'Instruments of Communion', developed to sustain and promote the life of the Anglican Communion, is now working in the way it was supposed to. Should people then simply 'learn to walk apart', as Windsor warned, each Province, or even diocese, looking to its own needs and opportunities? This is very far from the 'Mutual Responsibility and Interdependence' (MRI) and the 'Partners in Mission' processes which have, so far, characterised our common life together.[50]

Those Anglicans, in every province, who wish to uphold the authority of the Bible, the historic faith of the Church down the ages and the continuity of Apostolic order, have had to find ways of associating and of moving forward in the context of a confused world-wide Communion. Movements such as GAFCON (Global Anglican Future Conference) and the more diverse Global South, along with Catholic Anglican organisations like Forward in Faith, have come into

---

[49] *The Windsor Report* (London, ACO, 2004), pp 77ff. See also 'The Church of England's Response' in Michael Nazir-Ali and John Hind, *The Windsor Report, GS 1570* (London, Archbishops' Council, 2005) and Andrew Goddard, 'The Anglican Communion Covenant' in Ian S. Markham et al (eds), *Companion to the Anglican Communion* (Malden, MA, Wiley Blackwell, 2013), pp 119ff.

[50] *The Windsor Report*, p 75 and Coleman, *Resolutions of the Twelve Lambeth Conferences* pp 171ff etc.

existence to ensure that traditional understandings of Anglicanism are not simply extinguished under revisionist pressure.

4. Expressing the principles of Anglican heritage

We have been fortunate enough to inherit both the Sacred Deposit of Faith (of which Scripture is the norm) and a Sacred Ministry which is tasked with preaching the 'pure Word of God' and duly celebrating the Sacraments of the Church. In the history of the Church, there have been tendencies to emphasise one or other of these features of the Church – and this can result in complacency, faithlessness, division or even simply inaction. We need to adhere to both of these aspects of our faith and life, at the same time as making it quite clear that they are not on the same level. Although ministers are called of God and minister in his name, they are, nevertheless, always servants of the Word of God and never its masters.[51]

As we struggle to find fresh ways of expressing ourselves as 'church' or as a 'communion', we need to keep in mind what should characterise our life together. We need to find ways of gathering at every level of the Church's life – whether in the parish, at home, as a diocese or a national Church – or, indeed, across the Communion and world-wide. Naturally, such gatherings will be more than just meeting. They must be gatherings where the Word of God is at the centre. They will be prayerful and they will be Eucharistic, in the sense that we gather to give thanks for all God's goodness to us and to everyone, but specifically for his 'inestimable love in the redemption of the world by Our Lord Jesus Christ', as we say in the General Thanksgiving. When necessary, they will be about consulting one another regarding weighty matters confronting church and society. There will be times when the teaching of the Bible and the Church has to be clearly set out, to build up believers and as a witness to the world. Yes, there will also be occasions when the gathering is for sake of discipline, right doctrine and holy order in the Church. This is the proper meaning of being synodal (travelling together in the same way, as Ignatius says, "companions in festal procession along the way" – I Ephesians 9:2).

---

[51] See particularly Articles 20 and 26 of the *Articles of Religion* and '*Dei Verbum* 10', in Austin Flannery OP (ed), *Vatican Council II* (New York, Costello, 1987), pp 755f

Constitutions, bye-laws, rules of procedure and such like may or may not be necessary but we should never allow them to overshadow or to negate these vital aspects of 'walking together in the way of the Lord'.

4.1. A confessing church

At the level of the Communion, we need, once again, to affirm that we are a *confessing* Church. There is a widespread notion that Anglicans can believe anything and, sometimes, that they need believe 'nothing'. I have never been sure which is more dangerous! It is claimed, from time to time, that Anglicans are not 'confessional' in the sense of the great confessions of what has been called the 'Magisterial Reformation', whether the Augsburg Confession, the Westminster or the Zwinglian. This may be so but we should not forget that Anglicanism is irreducibly credal. We say the 'Catholic creeds'[52] perhaps more than any other Christian tradition: The Apostles' Creed at Morning and Evening Prayer, the Nicene at the Eucharist and even the 'Athanasian', if we follow the direction of the *Book of Common Prayer*. It is not enough, of course, simply to 'say' or sing the creeds. We should also be preaching the creeds, practising the creeds and praying the creeds. Only then can we become a truly believing church. From time to time, at the world-wide level also, the credal aspect of the Church will have to be put forward so that believers may know what they ought to believe and the world may know the faith of the Church.

4.2. A gathering church

It has been part of the Anglican genius to gather bishops, clergy and lay people in common concourse. There is great value in all parts of the Church listening to one another and receiving from one another, but such *synodal* or *conciliar* (to use another term) ways of gathering cannot just be undifferentiated mass meetings. We must take our cue from the earliest council of the Church, the Council of Jerusalem, the proceedings of which are reported in Acts 15:

- The Apostles and Elders (presbyters) consider the conditions of membership in the Church for gentiles coming to faith in Jesus Christ.

---

[52]   Cf Canon C15 of the Church of England, 'The declaration of assent', in which the creeds are so described.

- Peter and James declare what God is doing amongst the Gentiles and what is required for fellowship between Jewish and gentile Christians.

- The Apostles and Elders write the letter to the gentile brethren and the *whole church* chooses the people who are to represent them, with Paul and Barnabas, to the churches of the gentiles.

We see here a gathering of the whole Church but a *differentiated* gathering, i.e. different parts of the Body have, unsurprisingly, different functions to fulfil. Those who have been called to be the teachers of the faith, while always conscious of their own weakness (Joshua 3:1-5), should play a special part in any procedure where the Church is making decisions about faith, worship, the ordering of the ministry or questions about morality.

As Professor Owen Chadwick said at the 1988 Lambeth Conference, wherever there are bishops, they will find a way of coming together. This has, indeed, been the case from the beginning, with regional, provincial and patriarchal councils being held in addition to the generally recognised ecumenical councils. It should be noted, however, that although it was the bishops gathering, they were usually not alone, since they were assisted by clergy and lay people in their deliberations. For us, this should mean that bishops, and others with oversight, should be able to meet to discuss and to decide on those matters which especially pertain to their teaching, presiding and missionary office. Such meetings can take place within the context of a wider meeting such as GAFCON, or if necessary, be primarily meetings of bishops as at a Lambeth Conference. Such collegiality is not an end in itself but must always be at the service of the wider Church and, of course, of the Word of God itself. Its demand of loyalty must be determined by a common adherence to divinely revealed truth.

4.3. A disciplined church

Some of the Reformers were wary of ecclesiastical discipline because of their experience of excesses of discipline in the mediaeval Church. They soon discovered, however, that discipline was required if the Church was to stand and if it was to grow in holiness. Much discipline has to do with the 'cure of souls' and it is only when there is a consistent refusal to turn away from sin and repent, that sanction has to be applied. Where this results in exclusion from holding office or from the reception of sacraments, it can never extend to excluding anyone from hearing the Word of God. In any case, such exclusion must always be for the sake of restoration by God's grace and in his own time. It should have nothing to do with self-righteousness but should always be exercised in love and the readiness to forgive the repentant sinner.

The Anglican Reformers were clear in their affirmation of the need for discipline in the Church. Both the Articles and the Homilies show a concern for holiness of life and the discipline of clergy.[53] If the Body is to remain healthy, there is a need for discipline at every level of Church life, both in matters of faith and in the area of Christian behaviour and life-style. One of the problems in some churches in the West has been a lack of willingness to exercise discipline, and this has resulted in an unwillingness to be clear in teaching on doctrinal or moral issues.

In addition, then, to being confessing and conciliar, the Church has to be *consistorial*. This is a term not much used in Anglicanism but it signifies the need for proper mechanisms and processes if discipline is to be effective in the Church. In the Anglican Communion, proposals for the Covenant foundered on the unwillingness of some to countenance such effective measures for discipline. Without these, 'radical autonomy' will hold sway, and the Lambeth principle of an autonomy which nevertheless 'recognises the restraints of truth and love' will become impossible to maintain.[54]

4.4. A 'provisional' church

Successive Lambeth Conferences have expressed the willingness of Anglicanism to 'disappear' in the wider cause of Christian unity. They have expressed an openness to being less 'Anglican' so that the Church can be more 'catholic'. Indeed, in the national and regional unity schemes, such as those of South Asia, this is exactly what happened as Anglicans 'gave up' their identity for the sake of wider unity with brothers and sisters from other churches.[55] This commitment to provisionality raises two questions in our present situation:-

---

[53] Article 26 and the *Second Book of Homilies*, No 16 for Pentecost
[54] 'Encyclical, Lambeth Conference 1920' in Evans and Wright, *The Anglican Tradition*, p 383.
[55] For a summary of this acknowledgement of provisionality see *The Emmaus Report: A Report of the Anglican Ecumenical Consultation* (London, ACC, 1987), pp 11ff. See also Resolutions 50-65 of the 1948 Conference in Coleman, *Resolutions of the Twelve Lambeth Conferences* pp 101ff.

1. How does it apply to unity at the universal rather than just the regional level? Given the increasing dialogue between world communions, including the Anglican, this is a question that cannot be ignored.

2. Does provisionality apply not only to unity but also to truth? To what extent will a desire for truth lead us, more and more, to fellowship with those who share with us a passion for Gospel truth?

While the Conferences acknowledged the provisionality of Anglicanism, they also had a sense of its vocation for the wider Church.[56] Anglicans needed, of course, to receive from others but they also had gifts to bring to the wider fellowship. Anglican identity was, therefore, precious not so much for itself as for what it might mean for the world-wide Church of God. When pressed about this 'patrimony', Anglicans are sometimes hard put to it to enumerate its contents, but it would certainly include the order and beauty of Liturgy in the vernacular (a lasting gift of Archbishop Cranmer to the Church); the training and formation of clergy and the church's positive experience of both celibate and married clergy; an inductive, historical and biblical rather than scholastic theological temper; a tradition of pastoral care in the context of the wider community, local or national; and the involvement of lay people in consultation and decision-making. The list could, undoubtedly, be lengthened in the light of Anglican experience in different parts of the world. In any vision for the future of the Anglican Communion, it will be necessary to maintain this balance between a humble acknowledgement of provisionality and a confident affirmation of an identity which is seen to be providential and orientated towards others.[57]

5. Conclusion

We have seen how, in the course of history, mission has often come about through movements of people responding to God's call on their lives. The monastic movement in both East and West has been about

---

[56] Coleman, *Resolutions of the Twelve Lambeth Conferences*, p 105 and *The Emmaus Report*, p 15.

[57] See further Michael Nazir-Ali, 'The Anglican Communion and Ecumenical Relations' in Ian. S Markham et al (eds) *Companion to the Anglican Communion* (Wiley-Blackwell, Malden, MA, 2013), pp 581f.

the necessity of prayer, contemplation, simplicity and utter devotion, but it has also been about mission. Both individuals and religious orders have carried the faith far and wide. Mistakes have been made but there has also been courage, sacrifice and the extension of the kingdom of God through Christian presence and the proclamation of the gospel.[58]

The Evangelical revival resulted in, among other things, a recovery of the doctrine of means: that God uses human beings and their resources to further his work. This led to a veritable explosion of missionary concern and of vocations to world-wide and cross-cultural missions which, under God, has changed the map of the Christian world.[59]

Anglicans too have been influenced by the voluntary principle, both in their participation in inter-denominational missionary activity and in the use of specifically Anglican societies like the CMS, CMJ and, later, BCMS. We have seen also how the Tractarian movement became interested in mission, because of the possibility of missionary bishops planting churches that were more clearly catholic than the Erastianism of the Church of England would permit. Both CMS and UMCA, in different ways and at different times, became involved in campaigns against the slave trade and slavery itself. This gave a prophetic edge to their witness from the very beginning. Such a prophetic aspect to mission has been seen down the years, whether in the opposition to the caste system in India, or in the support of female education or in the resistance to racial segregation and apartheid in Southern Africa.

Once again, it is very likely that the renewal of Anglicanism will come about not through the reform of structures (necessary as that is), nor through institutional means, but through movements raised up by God. These can be mission movements for planting churches among the unreached, or movements for renewal in worship and for the receiving and using of God's gifts for the people. They can be campaigns for justice for the poor or for the persecuted. In many and varied ways the Gospel will, indeed, renew both the Church and the face of the earth.

---

[58] See further Neill, op. cit., pp 179ff; Timothy (Kallistos) Ware, *The Orthodox Church* (Harmondsworth, Middx, Penguin, 1973), pp 82ff, W.G. Young, *Patriarch Shah and Caliph* (Rawalpindi, Christian Study Centre, 1974), pp 121ff and Anton Wessels, *Europe: Was it Ever Really Christian?*, pp58ff.

[59] Michael Nazir-Ali, *From Everywhere to Everywhere*, p 46, Bebbington, *Evangelicalism in Modern Britain*, p 41

Because of the failure of the Instruments of Unity, we will also need movements which bring together orthodox Anglicans, whether provinces, dioceses, congregations or individuals. This will be for the sake of fellowship, for mutual support and for the renewal of the Communion as a whole. Some may, inevitably, develop an ecclesial dimension as they recognise provinces, dioceses and congregations as churches and as Anglicans. Such a sense of ecclesiality should never be schismatic in intention; but it arises out of necessity. It should lead to the modelling of an adequate ecclesiology, as outlined above, for the sake of the whole Communion and its future. No movement can be authentically ecclesial unless it is also missional and prophetic.

The Anglican Communion has emerged out of faithfulness to God's Word. It is built on the sacrifices and gifts of countless people. We believe it has a future under God but also that it needs, once again, to be reformed, renewed and equipped for its calling in today's world.

+Michael Nazir-Ali

October 2013

If you have enjoyed this book, you might like to consider

- *supporting the work of the Latimer Trust*
- *reading more of our publications*
- *recommending them to others*

  See www.latimertrust.org for more information.

Latimer Publications

Latimer Studies

Latimer Publications

Lightning Source UK Ltd.
Milton Keynes UK
UKHW040746180121
377122UK00009B/3